SHOW ME
Shipshewana

a Guide to Indiana Amish Country

THERESA L. GOODRICH

THE LOCAL TOURIST

Published in the United States by The Local Tourist

thelocaltourist.com

While every effort has been made to confirm the accuracy of the information contained within at time of publication, things change. Before visiting any of the destinations, attractions, accommodations, restaurants, etc., in this book, contact them to confirm.

ISBN: 978-1-958187-15-9

Also by Theresa L. Goodrich

Two Lane Gems, Vol. 1: Turkeys are Jerks and Other Observations from an American Road Trip

Two Lane Gems, Vol. 2: Bison are Giant and Other Observations from an American Road Trip

Living Landmarks of Chicago

Planning Your Perfect Road Trip

As Theresa L. Carter

Peril on the Peninsula

Revenge in the Rockies

Betrayed at the Beach

Publisher

Midwest Road Trip Adventures, 2nd Edition

Midwest State Park Adventures

Also by Theresa L. Goodrich

[illegible]

[illegible]

[illegible]

[illegible]

[illegible]

[illegible]

As Theresa L. Carter

[illegible]

[illegible]

[illegible]

Publisher

[illegible]

[illegible]

Contents

Introduction 1

Welcome to Indiana Amish Country 3

Know Before You Go 7

Indiana Amish Country FAQs 11

Tips for Driving in Amish Country 15

Meet the Amish 17

Discover the Towns of LaGrange County

- Meet the Communities 25

Exploring Amish Country

- Overview 37
- Off the Beaten Path Driving Tours 38

Outdoor Adventures

- Overview 42
- Cook's Bison Ranch 45

LaGrange County Parks 49

More Outdoors 52

Shopping

Overview 58

Shipshewana Flea Market 60

Shipshewana Miscellaneous & Antique Auction 67

Davis Mercantile 71

The Art of Quilting 77

Downtown Shipshewana 81

More Shopping 83

Arts & Entertainment

Overview 90

Blue Gate Music Hall and Blue Gate Performing Arts Center 92

Michiana Event Center 94

Murals of LaGrange County 95

Dining in LaGrange County

Overview 98

Blue Gate Restaurant and Bakery 100

Dinner in an Amish Home 103

Shipshewana Auction Restaurant 109
More Dining 111
Extend Your Trip 111
Where to Stay 111
Plan Your Adventure 113
Journal Pages 113

Introduction

Bite-sized guides; Buffet-sized adventures

Welcome to Show Me Shipshewana, The Local Tourist's guide to Indiana Amish Country.

Every place has stories. It's my passion to bring them to life, and I've been doing this a very, very long time: in 2002, I founded The Local Tourist as a guide to one neighborhood in downtown Chicago. Today, I cover travel all over the United States, specializing in road trips, the great outdoors, and unique destinations. I'm also a publisher and author of multiple books, most of which are themed around travel, even my fiction: my protagonist is a travel writer.

I've created this guidebook in partnership with LaGrange County Convention and Visitors Bureau. They pointed me in the right direction, introduced me to several of the people you'll meet in these pages, and covered my expenses. However, all opinions are expressly my own. The only things that influenced me were horses and pie, and lots of warm, welcoming people.

It's been my long-held belief that traveling to a place is not just about doing things. It's about truly experiencing a destination. Learning its stories. Meeting its residents. I want to help you go beyond the buggies and bonnets and discover the real Indiana Amish Country.

In this guide, you'll find both popular attractions and lesser-known spots, with both extensive profiles of my favorite places and directory-style listings to round out your planning.

> **TLTip:** Throughout this guide you'll see this term. It's to highlight a quick tip and is a play on the initials of my website, **T**he **L**ocal **T**ourist.

I hope this guide helps you experience the fascination of a tourist while feeling the comfort of the local.

Enjoy the journey, and have fun being a Local Tourist!

Theresa Goodrich

Welcome to Indiana Amish Country

Easy to Get to, Yet a World Away

In the northeast corner of Indiana, bordering Michigan and not quite to Ohio, is a land of farms and lakes. A highway runs through it. If you don't get off the interstate, you might think there's nothing to see.

Oh, how wrong you'd be.

Shipshewana and LaGrange County is an easy day trip from multiple large cities, but this is a place worth more than a quick visit. It's a place where you'll want to spend some time. Unwind. Relax. Disconnect from hectic daily life and try out a slower pace. You'll find miles of trails and acres of lakes, live entertainment, and all the shopping you can handle. Stock up on fresh produce and breathe in fresh air. You can feed bison and fill your belly, discover quilt barns and quilting bees. Enjoy the polished feel of beloved antiques and the sharp scent of new handmade furniture.

Welcome to Indiana Amish Country.

LaGrange County is the heart of Indiana Amish Country. To visit is to step into a simpler time, among people who live simply. Life is slower. Traffic jams involve buggies. Furniture is hewn from hardwood. Quilts are art. Even the food is simple: peanut butter, mashed potatoes, chicken and noodles, pie.

But simple doesn't mean boring. In Shipshewana and the surrounding communities, simple means intentional. The furniture is sturdy. Reclaiming and repurposing are a way of life. When it comes to the food, it also means delicious. There's a reason Amish cuisine is prized.

In a time of constant demands for our attention, of "hustle culture" and 24/7 access to information, of phones and tablets buzzing with notifications, of social media and apps and endless digital distractions, sometimes you just want to shut it all off and BE.

This is a place where you can do that. It's a place where you can ride an antique carousel, ride in a carriage, browse handmade quilts, see the mist rise off the fields in the morning and, in the evening, witness the sun dip to the horizon as a farmer drives a horse-drawn plow.

But a visit to Shipshewana and LaGrange County isn't all rocking chairs and pie (although if it were, that wouldn't be a bad thing).

It's also live entertainment, including concerts, musicals, and plays. It's shopping at the Midwest's largest flea market. It's petting farm animals and feeding the national mammal.

In this guide, we'll explore this fascinating area that's within three hours of several major cities and millions of people. You'll discover the Amish way of life, which is so intriguing to us "English." You'll learn the stories behind the towns of LaGrange County, including the feud that created a no-man's-land straight through Shipshewana.

And because reading about a place is great, but visiting is even better, you'll find practical guidance on things to do. There are driving tours, activities for outdoor adventurers, shopping galore, and arts and entertainment. You'll also find nearby attractions so you can extend your stay.

Before we get into the nitty gritty of planning your visit, we'll start with some things to know before you go: e.g. weather, location, time zone, etc. You'll find answers to your FAQs, and then it's a brief dive into Amish history and culture. There are in-depth profiles of my favorite places, and more directory-style listings of things to do, places to eat, and where to stay.

Because this is a guide to help you *plan* your vacation to Indiana Amish Country, there are itinerary planning pages. And, to help you remember your experience long after you've returned to the chaos of daily life, there's also space to record your memories.

Shipshewana, LaGrange County, and Indiana Amish Country are magical places inviting you to slow down, reconnect, and rejuvenate.

Are you ready? Enough chit-chat. It's time to Show YOU Shipshewana.

HARLEY D. YODER

Know Before You Go

Important Details for Planning Your Trip

Before you head to Shipshewana, there are a few essential details that will help you navigate your way through Indiana Amish Country. From the weather to local etiquette, here's a snapshot of what to expect.

Location

Shipshewana is located in LaGrange County, Indiana, near the Michigan border, and not quite reaching Ohio. It's easily accessible via I-90.

Time Zone

LaGrange County is in the Eastern Time Zone and follows Daylight Savings Time.

Population

As of the 2020 Census, LaGrange County had a population of

40,446 people. About 50% of its residents are Amish.

Weather

Shipshewana experiences a typical Midwestern climate with four distinct seasons:

- Spring: Mild with temperatures ranging from 40°F to 65°F.
- Summer: Warm, often humid, with highs around 75°F to 85°F.
- Fall: Cool and crisp, perfect for leaf-peeping, with temperatures from 45°F to 65°F.
- Winter: Cold with snowfall, temperatures ranging from 20°F to 35°F.

Best Time to Visit

- Spring and Fall: For milder weather and smaller crowds, consider visiting during these transitional seasons.
- Summer: Ideal for outdoor activities, but can be busier, especially during the Shipshewana Flea Market season.
- Winter: Perfect for a cozy getaway, especially if you enjoy snow-related activities.

Language

English is the primary language, though you may hear Pennsylvania Dutch spoken within the Amish community.

Currency

The U.S. Dollar (USD) is the currency used. Credit cards are widely accepted, but it's wise to carry some cash, particularly when visiting Amish-run businesses.

Dress Code

Casual and comfortable attire is appropriate. If visiting Amish businesses or attending community events, modest clothing is appreciated.

Connectivity

While most modern amenities are available, some Amish-owned establishments may not offer Wi-Fi. It's a perfect opportunity to unplug and enjoy the surroundings.

Etiquette

The Amish community values modesty, simplicity, and privacy. Respectful behavior and mindful photography (asking before taking photos) are appreciated.

Special Events and Festivals

Keep an eye on the local calendar for events such as quilt auctions, craft fairs, seasonal festivals, and other unique cultural experiences.

Visit Shipshewana

Don't forget to check out the voice of authority on all things La-Grange County. The LaGrange County Visitor's Bureau offers a wealth of information, and it's their passion to help you find things to do. Check out their website at visitshipshewana.org. Once you're in the area, say hi. Their visitor center is at 350 S. Van Buren Suite H, Shipshewana, IN, 46565 800.254.8090

Indiana Amish Country FAQs

Because the Amish intentionally separate themselves from modern-day life, there are many questions about them. Following are answers to some of the things that piqued my curiosity, as well as questions others have asked.

Do Amish speak with an accent?

Yes, many do because the Amish speak Pennsylvania Dutch in their homes and among each other.

Why are non-Amish called English?

Because their neighbors who aren't Amish generally speak English as their primary language.

What is rumspringa?

Delete any ideas of spring break for Amish from your mind. It's basically adolescence, and young Amish men and women are given more latitude to explore the world around them. Most end their rumspringa with the decision to be baptized. (More on that in the Meet the Amish chapter.)

Why do some Amish men have beards and others don't?

Amish men grow beards when they get married, although some will stop shaving when they decide to join the church. They continue to shave their mustaches, however, as those are considered ostentatious.

Do the Amish go to church?

Yes, the Amish attend church regularly, but it's not in a centralized institution. They gather in homes instead.

Can I visit an Amish church?

These are private, so no.

Do Amish kids go to school?

Yes. Generally speaking, Amish children attend school until the 8th grade. The Amish believe the point of an education is to earn a living and an eighth grade education is sufficient to do so.

Why don't the Amish want their photos taken?

Amish beliefs discourage having their photos taken because it's seen as a violation of the Second Commandment, which prohibits "graven images."

Can I visit Amish homes or farms?

You wouldn't just knock on someone's door, just like you wouldn't in any other destination. However, some Amish host dinners, like The Carriage House. Buggy Lane Tours and Stutzman Dairy Farm offer farm tours.

Why don't Amish people drive cars?

The Amish can drive cars, if necessary, but they choose not to, and they choose not to own them. This is because automobiles make it easier to spread apart, and the Amish value their families and communities.

Can I ride in a buggy?

Yes! There are tour companies that offer buggy rides, including Blue Gate Carriage, in front of the restaurant.

What are the sheds on the side of the road?

Those are Amish phone booths. The Amish don't keep telephones in their homes, so they install them in separate buildings.

Are those RV doors on the sheds?

Yes, they are! Many Amish men work at the RV factories in Elkhart County, and they use the doors for their sheds.

Are there specific traffic rules when sharing the road with horse-drawn buggies?

When encountering horse-drawn buggies on the road, slow down, give them plenty of space, and avoid startling the horses. Always obey traffic laws and be patient when driving in Amish Country. Check the next chapter for tips on driving in this area.

Is there a dress code for visitors?

There is no specific dress code for visitors, but dressing modestly is appreciated, especially when visiting Amish areas, out of respect for the local culture.

Can I use credit cards?

While many businesses accept credit cards, it's a good idea to carry cash. Smaller, Amish-owned shops and markets often only accept cash or check.

Are stores and restaurants open on Sunday?

Generally speaking, many businesses are closed on Sunday. This is especially true in the western part of the county, where the majority of the Amish live.

Tips for Driving in Amish Country

Because of LaGrange County's significant Amish population, you'll see lots of horse-drawn carriages and bicyclists. Be careful and aware while driving. Here are some tips to make driving in Amish country better for everyone.

- Take your time; pedestrians, buggies, and bikes are also sharing the road.

- Give yourself longer to brake—horses can't compete with automotive speed.

- Resist the urge to pass a buggy on curves or hills; it's not worth the risk.

- Give a buggy plenty of room at intersections; horses can reverse without warning.

- Be careful when overtaking a buggy; the driver's field of vision is quite limited.

- Horses are animals unpredictable. Exercise caution when nearing them.

- Keep an eye out for reflective markings on buggies, especially when driving at night.

Meet the Amish

Learn the Story Behind the Plain People

There are approximately 40,500 people in LaGrange County. Half of them are Amish.

While this community, which focuses on living simply and humbly, is a major tourist draw to the region (hence this book), many questions surround them. How did the Amish start? What does it mean to be Amish? Why do they live the way they do? And why are there so many of them in Northern Indiana?

The story of the Amish begins in the 16th century. It was a time of upheaval in Europe as the Protestant Reformation challenged the Catholic church's dominance. One group defied the concept of infant baptism, believing that baptism should be an informed choice made in adulthood. This didn't sit well with the powers that were, whether they were Protestant or Catholic. Labeled Anabaptists, which means *to rebaptize*, they were persecuted mercilessly. Hung, drowned, burned–thousands of Anabaptists were killed for their beliefs. Still, they continued, surviving and expanding their numbers.

Many of them followed Menno Simons, a Catholic priest who rejected the church in 1536 and became an influential figure among the Anabaptists. His followers became known as Mennonites. Another early Anabaptist, Jacob Hutter, was burned at the stake the same year Simons left the priesthood. The Hutterites shared similar beliefs, but they also held, and hold, all material goods in common.

Near the end of the 17th century, another influential man inspired a split. Jacob Ammann thought the Mennonites were getting to be too worldly. Today's Amish, his namesake, continue to live simple lives separate from the outside world and focused on family and community.

By the 18th century, Europeans had greatly expanded their reach in the Americas. In the early 1700s, William Penn, a Quaker, invited the Mennonites, Amish, and other religious groups to his "holy experiment." There, they found freedom and relief from persecution. The population grew, and some began migrating west, to Ohio, and eventually to Indiana.

Today, Pennsylvania, Ohio, and Indiana have the three largest populations of Amish, in that order.

TLTip: the Mennonites, Amish, and Hutterites are often called Plain People because of their modest clothing and simple living.

The first Amish arrived in LaGrange County in the early 1840s. They were drawn by the fertile soil and inexpensive land.

The world around them has changed dramatically, but the Amish continue to live simple and humble lives. They don't own vehicles or have electricity or telephones in their homes. They wear plain clothing. Even the food is simple (and delicious), with staples like chicken and noodles and mashed potatoes.

To an outsider, their lifestyle can seem incomprehensible. No cars, no phones, no–gasp–internet: how do they function?

Quite well, actually. The Amish are one of the fastest growing groups in the U.S. Part of that growth is because they consistently have families of five children or more. But a remarkable statistic is their 85% retention rate. To me, that indicates there's a lot to be said for their way of life.

At a simulated Amish wedding feast I attended, that's exactly how the host phrased it. "Being Amish is not a religion," he said. "It's a way of life."

Whether it's religion or not, their lives are informed by their faith, but they don't attend church in the traditional sense. There's no centralized authority. Several families create one congregation. They attend services in homes instead of dedicated buildings. Each congregation's bishop informs what technology is acceptable and in what form.

For example, when you drive through LaGrange County, you'll see lots of sheds with doors meant for recreational vehicles near the side of the road. Those are phone booths. The RV doors come from the nearby factories, which employ many Amish men. Amish are allowed to use the phone, just not in their homes. You'll also see solar panels, which power those phone booths. Their main forms of transportation are horse-drawn carriages and bicycles. They can ride in cars; they just can't own them.

Why? Every decision is based on the community and maintaining in-person interaction, and ensuring that the adoption of anything new doesn't disintegrate their connections.

When you visit LaGrange County, it's easy to recognize the Amish. The women wear dresses and aprons. The men wear pants with suspenders and shirts of solid colors. Women pull their hair back into a bun, which is covered by their bonnet. Married men grow beards, but shave their moustaches, as those are considered ostentatious. Men and boys wear wide-brimmed, flat-topped hats made either of straw or black felt.

You'll also see Mennonites, but it's often hard to tell them apart. Today's Mennonites, like their predecessors who prompted Jacob Ammann to split, are more worldly.

Whether you encounter someone who's Amish or Mennonite, the main thing to remember is to be respectful and polite (which is good advice for interacting with others, period). Their way of life is attractive and is a tourist attraction; however, *they* are not tourist attractions. They are people. As Elaine Jones, who hosts in-home Amish dinners told me, "We're still human."

One of your first stops when you visit Indiana Amish Country should be **Menno-Hof**. Labeled an "information center" instead of a museum, the non-profit tells the stories of the Anabaptists, from their origins in Switzerland to the Mennonites, Amish, and Hutterites of today.

Menno-Hof opened in 1988, prompted by the many questions attendees of the Shipshewana Flea Market had about the local population. An old-fashioned barn raising drew two-hundred volunteers to construct the building.

> **TLTip:** The name Menno-Hof is derived from Menno Simons and Hof, the German word for farmstead.

Inside, Menno-Hof takes you through five centuries of history, but it's not done in a dry manner. Instead, you'll sit in a medieval dungeon, explore a 17th century ship, and see what a 19th century printing shop was like. You can experience what a tornado feels like, and view a replica of an Amish home.

Menno-Hof is open Monday through Saturday. Tours last about an hour and fifteen minutes. It's located on State Road 5 (South Van Buren) across the street from the flea market and down the road from the Visit Shipshewana visitors' center.

Menno-Hof

510 S. Van Buren Shipshewana, IN 46565, 260.768.4117
menno-hof.squarespace.com

Discover the Towns of LaGrange County

NO
ENTER

Meet the Communities

The stories behind the towns.

Each town in LaGrange County has its own distinct character. Shipshewana is a marketplace of Amish craftsmanship, where you can hear an auctioneer's staccato and the rhythmic clip-clop of horse-drawn buggies. In Howe, you can play a round of golf and shoot a bow and arrow. Head to Mongo for outdoor adventures on the Pigeon River. LaGrange is the county's cornerstone; its court-house is on the National Register of Historic Places. Wolcottville is a respite of tranquil lakes and a bison ranch while in Topeka, farms stretch to the horizon.

Each town has its own vivid story, intricately linked to the others, yet still unique.

LaGrange County is a decidedly rural destination. The area is covered in farmland and these small towns dot the landscape, none with a population higher than 3000. With I-90 running through it and easy access to multiple metropolitan areas, it seems like this is an intentional decision, especially when you consider the county directly west is the RV capital of the world.

Modern day LaGrange County–which is almost an oxymoron due to its high Amish population–began when the first white settlers arrived. The Potawatomi inhabited the area, including a chief named Shipshewana. In 1828, Nathan Fowler built his cabin on Crooked Creek, near a Potawatomi settlement called Mongoquinong. More and more people moved in, a great migration from New England and other eastern states. They established Elkhart County in 1830, and two years later, carved out what became LaGrange County.

Entire families migrated. In 1833, John B. Howe opened the first school with twenty students. Towns formed. Moses and Ica Rice laid out the town of Mongoquinong in 1834. Daniel Harding built the first sawmill a year later. The next year, Drusus Nichols opened a distillery. In 1837, George Wolcott built a log cabin, then a sawmill, then a grist mill.

All this industry meant only one thing for the Potawatomi, and in 1838, they were forcibly removed. This Death March, as it became known, included Chief Shipshewana. He was so broken-hearted he returned the next year and remained until his death in 1841. He's reportedly buried near Shipshewana Lake.

I've read several histories of LaGrange County from the early 1900s and before, and they're all written in a similar style. They focus on the development of each township and the individuals who built them. It's almost as if each township, and its towns, is an island.

And yet they're also connected. To explore LaGrange County is to see several independent and interdependent communities. This is evidenced in the large Amish population, which began arriving in the early 1840s. Today they may live separately, but with their interest and influence in tourism, they still interact with the "English," which is how they refer to non-Amish because they speak English as their primary language.

While I could write a whole book solely about the history of this area, I'm going to stick with a brief recap of each town's founding and early years. I know you want to explore the LaGrange County of today, but after this section, you'll have a better understanding of how it came to be.

The towns are in chronological order based on when they were platted.

Howe

Population: 610

Howe's been through a few name changes in its storied history. It began as Mongoquinong, which was the Potawatomi name when the first white settlers arrived in 1828. That name may mean Big Squaw Village. It may have been the name of a chief. And, it may have been the name of the area. When brothers Moses and Ica Rice, who'd arrived in 1829, platted the town in 1834, they named it Mongoquinong. Moses and Ica wanted their town to be the county seat, and they donated 74 acres to make that happen.

It did, but their name didn't stick. Two years later, the Indiana House of Representatives passed an act changing the town to Lima. At the time, most of the settlers lived in the northern part of the county. By 1844, that had shifted south, so the county seat was moved to LaGrange.

One of the pioneers was John B. Howe. In 1833, he opened the first public school in LaGrange County about a quarter mile southeast of Lima, which was still Mongoquinong. Education was important to the attorney, and when he died in 1883, his bequest was used to found the Howe School. The next year, the community named the town for him.

In 1895, Howe School became the Howe Military Academy. It closed in 2019, but several properties on the former academy's grounds are listed on the National Register of Historic Places, including the John Badlam Howe Mansion.

LaGrange

Population: 2,715

LaGrange is the county's largest town and the county seat. Named for the country home of the Marquis de Lafayette, four early settlers platted the town in 1836 after buying the land from the U.S. Government. When the legislature moved the county seat from Lima to LaGrange, they needed a new courthouse and erected a frame building. In 1878-1879, a gorgeous red brick building with a clock tower and mansard roofs became the center of town. The building is on the National Register of Historic Places and is the centerpiece of a downtown decorated with murals and featuring several restaurants.

Mongo

Population: 102

The first time I read about the towns of LaGrange County, I noticed that two of them claimed to formerly be named Mongoquinong. Of course, I assumed that was a mistake, which goes to show you can't assume anything. Mongo, which is southeast of Howe, formerly Lima, formerly Mongoquinong, is a miniscule town of maybe a hundred people. Yet, its post office dates back to 1832, making it one of the earliest, if not the earliest, post office in the county. According to *From Needmore to Prosperity: Hoosier place names in folklore and history*, the post office was established at the site of a French fur trading post. By 1833, L. K. Brownell had built a grist mill and a distillery. John O'Farrell opened a trading store, and Arthur Burrows opened a hotel. Drusus Nichols laid out the town of Mongoquinong in 1840, four years after the previous Mongoquinong became known as Lima.

Mongoquinong was shortened to Mongo in 1874. Today this tiny town is known for its access to the Pigeon River and for a tasty pork burger at the general store.

Wolcottville

Population: 1,004

In June 1834, Peter Lampson and Nelson Nichols grabbed the first land claims in an area filled with lakes. John Adams claimed his own land in November of that year, next to a lake that would later be named for him. But Wolcottville is named what it is because of a settler who arrived in 1837. He built a log house and kept building. He built a saw mill, a grist mill, a carding mill—no wonder the town, laid out in 1849 and platted in 1853, became known as Wolcotts Mills.

In addition to mills, George also built the Wolcott Seminary.

George didn't live very long; he died in 1857 at just 51 years old. The town became Wolcottville, pronounced Wool-ca-ville, in 1864. Today this town, which is only 1.02 square miles, is surrounded by lakes and parks and home to Cook's Bison Ranch.

Shipshewana

Population: 839

LaGrange County's most well-known town is Shipshewana. Compared to some of the other spots, it got a late start. The town, named for Chief Shipshewana, wasn't platted until 1889, and getting there was quite the battle.

Two settlers each accumulated a lot of land in the western part of the county. These neighbors owned a combined 1900 acres: Abraham Summey claimed 500 on the west side of the road, and Hezekiah Davis owned 1400 on the east. If they'd been content with farming, everything might have been fine. But these two were a bit more ambitious. They each wanted to start a town, at the same time. So they did.

Summey named his town Summey Town. Davis called his Davis Town. Summey sold lots and had buildings face the street that divided the towns. Davis, however, left a swath 150-feet wide empty and prohibited anyone from building, creating a distinct separation. Then Hezekiah had the brilliant idea to bring the railroad through Davis Town. He paid $10,000, the railroad came through, and Summey Town ceased to exist.

There's little mention of Abraham Summey in the histories of LaGrange County. He doesn't even merit inclusion in *LaGrange County Centennial History, 1828-1928* and there's only one reference to him in *History of Northeast Indiana*, and that's concerning the Congregational Church at Ontario. He gets the most ink on the Town of Shipshewana's website and on an historical marker located across from the former train depot.

In a surprising twist, the Summey and Davis families had a Romeo and Juliet ending to their feud. Hezekiah's son Eugene married Abraham's daughter Alice. And the author of the tribute to the two men on this historical marker? Doris Davis. I checked out the family tree, and it wouldn't surprise me to learn she was the same Doris Davis that was Eugene and Alice's granddaughter.

So what happened to Davis Town? Hezekiah's wife, Sarah, suggested they name the new community Shipshewana and it was founded in 1889. That same year he founded the Bank of Shipshewana. Hezekiah died in 1891, a mere two years after he got his town, and Sarah continued to run the bank with their son Hewlitt.

When you visit Shipshewana today, in addition to the historical marker, there's a mural dedicated to Hezekiah Davis. Since you'll be right next door to Davis Mercantile, step inside and look for a shop on the first floor called Sarah Davis, after the influential woman.

Topeka

Population: 1,206

If you've gotten the idea that folks in LaGrange County liked to change the names of their towns, you'd be right. Topeka began in 1837 as Haw Patch, named for its abundance of hawthorn trees. The area was known for its rich, fertile, and level land, making it perfect for cultivating. In addition to hawthorns, oak, hickory, and black walnut covered the area.

At first, Haw Patch didn't refer to a town, but instead to a swath of land around 4,000 acres. Despite its agricultural appeal, according to *Counties of LaGrange and Noble, Indiana: Historical and Biographical* from 1882, in the early years of the county the area harbored "horse-thieves and general outlaws," which made the Haw Patch an "unsafe and disagreeable place." By 1858, the good upstanding citizens had enough, and formed the Regulators of Haw Patch. In an example of frontier justice, these Regulators caught one of the criminals, hung him, and sent the body back to his wife. The Regulators continued making arrests and "in a very short time the county was quiet."

The land itself was a big draw for the Amish, and they began settling in the area. You'll see the names of those early settlers today, including Bontrager and Yoder. The town of Haw Patch was platted at the end of 1891. In 1893 the name changed to Topeka, because railroad officials thought the Haw Patch resembled the Kansas city.

Exploring Amish Country

Michigan St

Overview

It's time to start exploring!

I've broken down the many things to do into categories to make it easy to plan your trip based on your interests.

We'll start with a suggested driving tour, which gives you the lay of the land as you hunt for barn quilts. Then you'll find outdoor adventures, with plenty of places for hiking, fishing, and even practicing your archery.

You'll quickly learn that shopping in LaGrange County isn't just about buying; it's about engaging with a culture rich in craftsmanship and heritage. In the Arts & Entertainment section, you'll discover venues offering both big-name performers and shows you won't find elsewhere. Finally, I'll introduce you to the best dining in the area.

Are you ready to explore Indiana Amish Country? Let's go!

Off the Beaten Path Driving Tours

What better way to get the lay of the land than to *see* the land. Take a driving tour and go on a rural scavenger hunt, searching for barn quilts and Amish shops while exploring the beautiful Indiana countryside.

The Barn Quilt Trail starts in Shipshewana and connects six communities around the county. Many of these colorful squares are on the sides of barns, as you'd expect, and others are in more unexpected places, like a log cabin in a campground.

Begun as a way to enhance the Shipshewana Quilt Festival, the Trail is now a draw on its own. It's simultaneously thrilling and relaxing to drive past farms and fields and encounter one of these works of art.

The history of barn quilts dates back to early Pennsylvania immigrants. It's said the patterns were used to celebrate heritage as well as navigational tools. Since 2001, they've become increasingly popular.

As you're driving from one town to the next to find the next quilt, take some time to stop at one of the many county parks, grab a bite to eat, and maybe even row on the Pigeon River for a bit.

You could also go shopping. If you see a sign selling crafts, baked goods, or other items, feel free to pull over–unless it's a Sunday.

Amish goods are another reason people visit LaGrange County, and the Amish Shop Trail makes it easy to find them. There are bakeries, a creamery, wood products, leather stores, general stores, and many other places to find these handcrafted goods. This trail is primarily on the western side of the county, where the concentration of Amish live.

Navigating the county is fairly simple, as there are several north-south and east-west roads. Everything starts with US 20 and State Road 9. East and West roads are oriented around SR 9, and the dividing line for North and South roads is US 20. Each 100 is one mile. So 100 North means 1 mile north of US 20.

Easy, right?

There are a few diagonal and curved roads, but for the most part, it's easy to get around.

You can download a map featuring all the stops on both of these trails, as well as additional places to eat and drink, at visitshipshewa na.org. If you're looking for a cocktail during your stay in LaGrange

County, this map will come in handy: it lists several taverns and bars.

I also recommend picking up a paper map at the visitor's center. And while you're there, you can check one of those barn quilts off your list.

Outdoor Adventures

Overview

Get outside and explore the beautiful Indiana countryside

One of the best ways to slow down is to get outside. Fortunately, there are plenty of opportunities for enjoying Mother Nature in LaGrange County. As you're driving along the backcountry roads, searching for quilt barns or Amish cottage shops, you'll find hiking trails, public beaches, lakes just waiting for your fishing rod, and even an archery range.

There's also a bison ranch, where you can feed the nation's mammal, and an animal park where you can meet—and feed – all sorts of other creatures. History buffs will love discovering pioneer log buildings which have been relocated from around the county. You can go canoeing, kayaking, and hunting, and ride your bike.

With nearly two-dozen lakes and miles of trails, if your idea of a great vacation includes some time in the fresh air, LaGrange County's got you covered.

Bison
Ford

Cook's Bison Ranch

Feed the Bison at This Agritourism Destination

If you've been to any place where there are bison, you've heard the admonitions: stay away from the bison, and whatever you do, don't try to feed the bison. This is for good reason. Bison are giant. They are massive animals who are not only big, they're also fast. This makes them dangerous. There's a reason every park with free-roaming bison posts warning signs. Get too close, and you could regret it.

This is not the case at Cook's Bison Ranch. Located in Wolcottville in the southeast part of the county, this family farm invites you to get up close and personal with the massive beasts.

They'll even let you feed them.

The foundations of Cook's Bison Ranch date back to 1939. That's when Peter Cook's grandfather Everett bought 83 acres, a house, and a barn for $5,000. The newlywed's father-in-law thought it was an awful decision, but he did it anyway.

He proved him wrong, paying back the loan with "two good years of popcorn." Everett created a successful business that he passed down to his son, Wayne.

The farm focused on cattle, crops, and chicken, but after several family trips to Wyoming and Yellowstone National Park, Everett's grandson Peter had fallen in love with the wooly mammal. He joined the National Bison Association. He researched. And, eventually, he convinced Wayne that raising bison would be a good idea. In 1998, they got their first 30 head and the family farm became a bison ranch.

Bison need room to roam, and the Cooks have the land. There's lots of grass for them to feed on, and there's no danger of them going hungry. Understanding that others, like Peter, are also fascinated by the USA's National Mammal, they also offer tours.

Erica Cook, co-owner of the ranch and Peter's wife, took me out with the bison on a blue-sky day. She fired up the antique tractor and I rode behind her in a covered wagon. The bison had been milling about in an enclosure, but as soon as she opened the gate and drove through, the herd joined us. Some ran ahead, racing towards the open field. Others trailed behind. And some trotted along beside us.

There were bulls and cows and calves. Riding in the wagon alone was a thrill; the closest I'd ever been to bison before was while camping at Badlands National Park. I stood on one side of my vehicle, parked on the gravel road that circled Sage Creek Campground, while they grazed on the other side of the road. But riding in the Cook's wagon, the bison were close enough to touch.

Erica had given me a bag of pellets so I could feed them. At first I was nervous. The warnings against getting too close to these creatures are indelibly etched in my brain. Erica stayed on the tractor, standing on the seat to talk with me. She told me she never gets down and walks among them. Even though their herd seemed docile, these are still wild, unpredictable animals with an innate sense of curiosity. I imagine they'd give "don't know my own strength" a whole new meaning.

I grabbed a few pellets and dropped them, aiming for their tongues. I missed, every time, and they dropped into the tall grasses. Erica told me not to worry. They don't have great eyesight, but they do have a great sense of smell and they'd be able to find them. Finally, I extended my arm further out and the beautiful beast wrapped the longest tongue I've ever seen around my hand.

Did you know bison tongues are scratchy?

Eventually, I even pet one with one hand while feeding it with the other. I felt giddy, a child-like thrill. It wasn't only because it seemed like I was breaking the rules–don't touch the bison, and don't *ever* feed them rang in my head–it was also because they truly are magnificent. I could understand how Peter could fall so in love with them they'd change the course of his and Erica's lives.

You can experience that thrill yourself and take a tour. Check their website or call ahead. While they do offer some open tours that don't require reservations, Cook's Bison Ranch is a working ranch, so those are limited and only available seasonally.

This agritourism destination offers multiple types of private group tours, including a Ranch Tour, a BBQ Chuckwagon Tour, a BBQ Chuckwagon Dinner Tour, and a Bison Burger Meal Tour.

Before you go, spend some time in the gift shop. You can pick up some bison meat, some bison jerky, and plenty of souvenirs.

Cook's Bison Ranch

5645 E 600 S Wolcottville, IN 46795, 260-854-3297
cooksbisonranch.com

LaGrange County Parks

LaGrange County has plenty of parks and nature preserves, offering a variety of experiences. Started in 1969, the LaGrange County Department of Parks & Recreation has carefully developed a series of outdoor settings that mix cultural richness with nature's beauty.

These ten park properties include public beaches, nature preserves, and lots of opportunities for outdoor recreation, including archery and disc-golf.

TLTip: Foraging is allowed in LaGrange County Parks.

You can pick mushrooms, berries, and nuts. (But please leave flowers and plants.)

Formerly a YMCA camp, **Dallas Lake Park** has a public swimming beach, a playground, and a 1.75-mile accessible walking trail. There's a wetlands observation deck overlooking Pond Lil, which is a state nature preserve. Admission is $5 (car, buggy, or motorcycle) and there's an honor box at the entrance.

Nearby, **David Rogers Memorial Park** is for the history buff. This park celebrates Dr. Rogers, one of the county's philanthropic pioneers who was also an herb doctor and a naturalist. He passed in 1871 and is buried on-site. The park takes you back in time with a reconstructed village, featuring seven historic log buildings that include homes, a barn, a smokehouse, and a performance stage.

Delt Church Park was the county's first park, donated in 1933. Located next to the Little Elkhart River, it's a favorite spot for locals, especially among the Amish community. There's a large playground and two miles of accessible trails, and bicycles are allowed. There's also the area's only 18-hole disc golf course. Need equipment? Stop by the Park Office at Dallas Lake Park for a starter kit. If you want to cook out, they've got charcoal grills.

Duff Memorial Park is a wetlands area on the south shore of Cedar Lake. There are no amenities, because its focus is habitat preservation.

Maple Wood Nature Center is where education meets exploration. Built shortly after a land donation in 1985 for the LaGrange County Nature Preserve, the Nature Center has become a vital community resource. It hosts the annual "Maple Syrup Days," giving locals and visitors a firsthand experience in the age-old craft of syrup-making. The center has expanded to include more land, additional learning spaces, and even a neighboring trail system.

With 254 acres, **Pine Knob Park** is the largest property in the LaGrange County parks portfolio. It began humbly as a 59-acre gift, its caretaking legacy handed over by the Pine Knob Conservation Club to ensure ongoing restoration and preservation. There are two lakes—Meteer and Duff—where you can go fishing, and a 3D archery trail. The Mike Metz Fen Trail winds around Duff Lake.

A few minutes northwest of Shipshewana is **Shipshewana Lake Park**. This pocket park has a shelter and a playground. The picnic area is lakeside.

There are three additional public beaches: Atwood Lake Beach, Wall Lake Beach, and Cedar Lake Beach. Also on Cedar Lake is the Cedar Fen, a 31-acre refuge for endangered wildlife.

All park hours are 8:00am to Sunset. Note: alcoholic beverages are prohibited in all LaGrange County Parks.

LaGrange County Parks

0505 W 700 S Wolcottvile, IN 46795, 260.854.2225

lagrangecounty.org

More Outdoors

Looking for even more ways to get outside? Whether you prefer the hands-on experience of a family-friendly animal park, the serenity of canoeing or kayaking down clear rivers, the thrill of hunting and fishing in a dedicated preserve, or the simple pleasure of a long bike ride on a scenic trail, you'll find it in LaGrange County.

Feed More Animals

Dutch Creek Farm Animal Park is a hands-on animal park where you can feed a variety of species from deer to zebras. Ideal for families, it offers educational animal shows and a petting zoo area. You can tour the entire farm in your own vehicle or via a horse-drawn wagon. If you want to feed the animals, the wagon's the way to go.

Dutch Creek Farm Animal Park

6255 N 1000 W Shipshewana, IN 46565, 260.768.4416
dutchcreekfarmanimalpark.com

Paddle Down the River

LaGrange County's a paddler's paradise. The Fawn River is one of Indiana's clearest and most natural rivers, and it flows through the northern part of LaGrange County. T & L Country Canoes will rent you canoes or kayaks so you can enjoy some time on the water and see unspoiled country. You can rent a vessel for as little as an hour (min. 2 vessels) or up to seven hours.

Head to Mongo and Trading Post Outfitters and travel through the Pigeon River Fish and Wildlife Area. They offer four different trips, including one that's for thirteen miles and meant for experienced paddlers. They also have a beautiful campground on the Pigeon River with both primitive sites and those with hookups.

T & L Country Canoes

5775 W 750 N Shipshewana, IN 46565, 260.562.2411
tlcountrycanoesllc.com

Trading Post Outfitters

7525 E 300 N Mongo, IN 46771, 260.367.2493
tradingpostcanoe.com

Hunt and Fish

Pigeon River Fish and Wildlife Area is nearly 12,000 acres, including seventeen miles of free-flowing river. A dedicated area for hunting and fishing, the preserve requires a state license for both activities. It offers a variety of fish, including smallmouth and largemouth bass, and game such as deer, pheasant, wild turkey, and waterfowl. There's also a shooting range.

If you just want to view the wildlife, head to the L2 parking lot and the Waterfowl Resting Area overlook. Canoeing and kayaking are permitted, but some areas are restricted during waterfowl season.

Like LaGrange County parks, foraging for mushrooms, berries, and nuts is allowed.

Pigeon River Fish and Wildlife Area

8310 E 300 N Howe, IN 46746, 260.367.2164
on.IN.gov/pigeonriverfwa

Hike or Bike

Want some exercise after indulging in JoJo's Pretzels at Davis Mercantile? Walk a couple blocks to the Pumpkinvine Nature Trail. The Pumpkin Vine Railroad, so named because of its twists and turns, served the area for a century before shutting down in 1980. Today, it's a paved biking and walking trail that stretches from Goshen through Middlebury to Shipshewana. Its nearly seventeen miles pass through farmlands and forests, offering both scenery and a well-maintained path.

Pumpkinvine Nature Trail

PO Box 392 Goshen, IN 46527
pumpkinvine.org

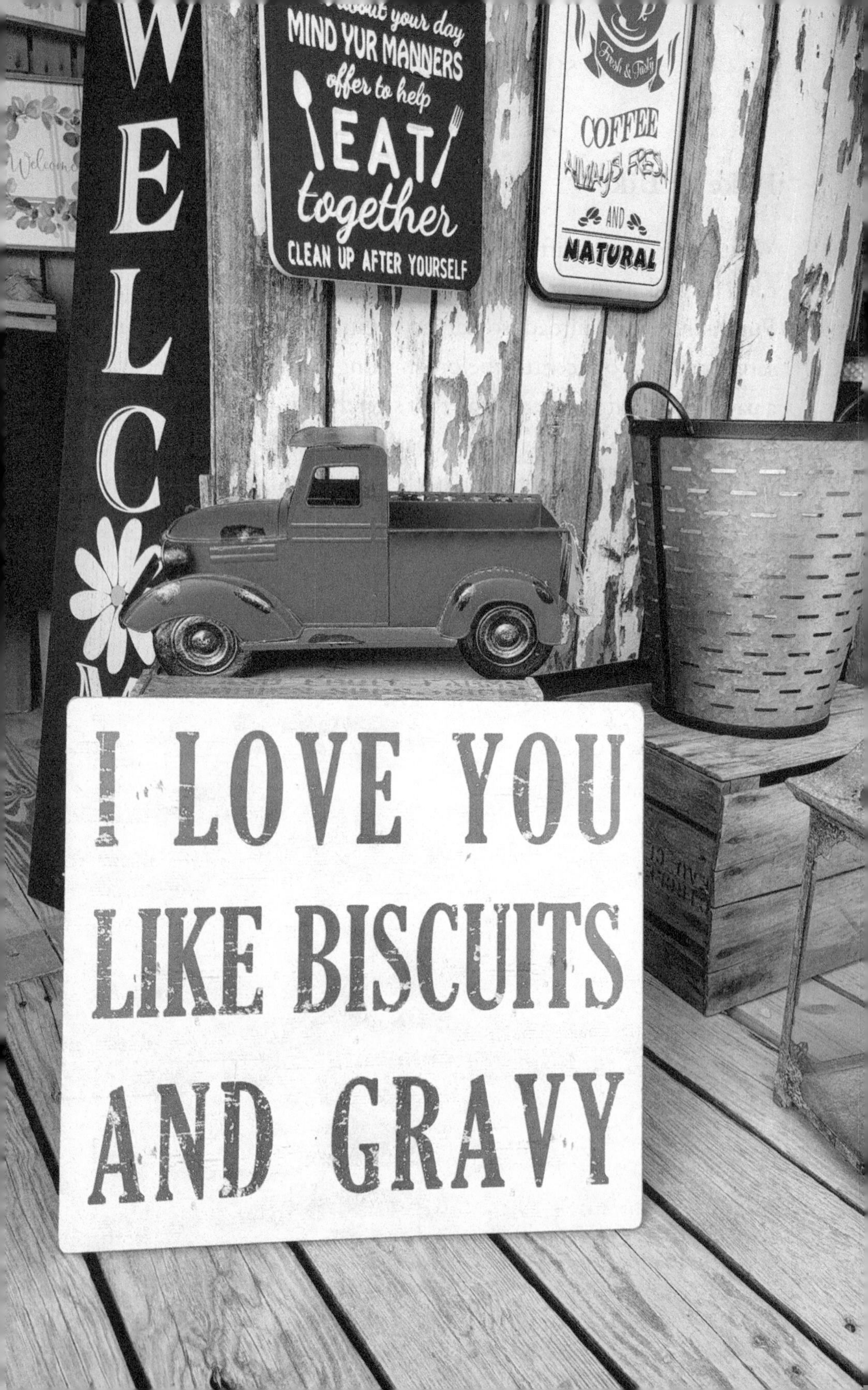
WELC
about your day
MIND YUR MANNERS
offer to help
EAT
together
CLEAN UP AFTER YOURSELF
Fresh & Tasty
COFFEE
ALWAYS FRESH
AND
NATURAL
I LOVE YOU
LIKE BISCUITS
AND GRAVY

Shopping in LaGrange County

Overview

Antiques, Handmade Items, and the Midwest's Largest Flea Market

Shopping in Shipshewana is a true delight, even if, like me, you don't consider yourself a shopper. This is a place where commerce intertwines with culture and tradition. Here, the act of buying and selling is not just a transaction; it's a connection between the visitor and the community.

The area's known for the Shipshewana Flea Market, the largest flea market in the Midwest. Another must-stop is Davis Mercantile, with its soft pretzels, vintage carousel, and four floors of shops in the heart of downtown. It's surrounded by local businesses, including Rebecca Haarer Arts and Antiques. Specializing in antique quilts, when you take something home from this shop, you're getting a piece of the community.

After reading about these places, you'll understand why shopping in Shipshewana is less about buying stuff and more about exploration, discovery, and connecting with a community that takes pride in its work and heritage. Whether you leave with full bags or simply with memories and insights, the experience is unique and enriching.

One important note: Shipshewana closes down on Sundays. If shopping is part of your itinerary, plan to visit the other days of the week.

SHIPSHEWANA FLEA MARKET

THE MIDWEST'S LARGEST FLEA MARKET

Each week between May and September, about ten- to twelve-thousand people flock to the tiny town of Shipshewana, Indiana. While there, they might take in a show. They'll probably eat some Amish peanut butter. They'll definitely see horse-drawn buggies, women in bonnets, and men wearing straw hats.

And they'll go shopping at the Shipshewana Flea Market.

The Midwest's largest flea market has been a destination for over a century. Today it's part of Shipshewana Trading Place, a sprawling collection of businesses dedicated to bringing buyers and sellers together.

With nearly 700 vendors, the number of people working the market exceeds the town's population. The number of people attending exceeds the population of many Midwestern towns.

Why is this flea market such a big draw? Why do so many people come from not only all over the Midwest, but all over the country, to shop at a flea market?

The short story is that it's a high quality market with an enormous variety of goods, great food, and a longstanding history.

I visited the market on a Wednesday morning, arriving early enough to see the chaos that is the Shipshewana auction. Then I walked up and down the aisles of vendors. For hours. I think I got my steps for the entire week in one morning.

The people watching alone is grand. You're in Indiana Amish Country, so there are Amish and Mennonites at the market. There are also those thousands of people, and they come from every walk of life. The scents are mouth-watering (once you get far enough away from the livestock barn). Fresh-baked pretzels, kettle corn, fudge, barbecued chicken - it's enough to make my mouth water just remembering it.

Visually, it's like trying to focus on Seurat's *A Sunday on La Grande Jatte* when you're standing too close. There's simply too much to make sense of it all. A patio table that spins like a lazy susan (which is brilliant, by the way)? Suits of armor? Antique meat grinders and a cape that looks like a cow?

You can buy it all at the Shipshewana Flea Market.

The Story of the Shipshewana Flea Market

The earliest recorded use of the term flea market is 1922. Coincidentally (or not), that's the date the Shipshewana Flea Market began.

Technically, one of the best flea markets in the United States didn't start in 1922, but it can trace its beginnings to that date. That's when George Curtis held his first livestock auction. He sold six pigs, seven cows, and several head of young cattle. That modest beginning became a weekly affair that continues to this day.

The auction continued to grow and after eight years, Curtis decided people would want to eat, so he turned his garage into a restaurant. Women from the Methodist Church would come over each week and cook for those hungry buyers and sellers. A decade later, Milo and Ruth Miller took over the feeding responsibilities. Before they could even get started, they'd have to back Curtis's car out of the garage, tidy it up, and then set up their equipment. Ruth brought home-baked pies, fresh from her own oven, and vegetables fresh from her garden. Diners could get burgers for twenty cents and top them with her homemade catsup.

In 1947, Curtis sold the auction to Fred Lambright. With the auction came a pop-up flea market. People showed up for the auction with cars full of stuff to sell. They'd pop their trunks and the exchange would begin. That same year, Lambright built a roof for the market, but people continued to sell out of their cars. All these people needed to eat, and they outgrew the garage. In 1950, Lambright opened the Auction Restaurant, which could seat up to sixty people.

The Shipshewana auction was sold for a third time in 1961 when Walter Schrock bought it. By this time, people were no longer selling out of their cars. It was a bona fide flea market, and he expanded it to 400 vendors. During Schrock's tenure, he also built the Antique Auction Building, which is where the Shipshewana Miscellaneous and Antique Auction is held every Wednesday. He had to rebuild the livestock auction barn after a fire destroyed the original.

Schrock owned the auction, flea market, and restaurant for twenty years before selling it to Fred Lambright's son. Robert Lambright expanded the outdoor flea market to a whopping 1000 spaces, opened a new sit-down restaurant, and built an office building. That many vendors, plus the crowds searching for bargains, or that perfect item, needed a place to stay. In 1997, Lambright opened the Farmstead Inn. Located directly across the street from the flea market, it's the most convenient accommodation for vendors and buyers.

From 1998 to 2017, shoppers could look for classic pieces at the Shipshewana Antique Mall. The building is now the Farmstead Expo Barn and is primarily used for special events and auctions. Today, the little auction that Curtis started and Schrock and the Lambrights built is the Midwest's largest flea market, and Fred's grandson Keith Lambright runs it all.

Considering it's one of the biggest flea markets in the country, it's easy to be overwhelmed with the sheer number and variety of choices. There's everything from perfume to home décor to wooden flamingos. There's a farmer's market selling fresh produce. There are vintage items, handmade items, collectibles, and antique furniture.

Fortunately, you can see the vendors online and plan your adventure. They've also got various "trails" so you can focus on specific types of merchandise. A fun trail is the "Flea Bag Trail." This scavenger hunt challenges you to visit specific vendors, locate the sign (hint: it's by the cash registers), and count the number of fleas. You'll jot that number down and the vendor will punch your card. Visit all of them, and you'll get a souvenir bag.

Another fun thing to do is mine for gems. The Gem Mining Sluice is near the entrance.

Tips for visiting Shipshewana Flea Market

The Shipshewana Flea Market runs on Tuesdays and Wednesday, May through September, from 8 am to 4 pm. You could spend the entire day at this bargain hunters' paradise. Whether that's your plan or you just want to browse for a couple of hours, here are some tips for making the most out of your experience.

Wear comfy shoes. At over 40 acres, this open-air market is huge.

Bring cash. While some vendors take credit cards, some do not. The split's about fifty-fifty.

Come prepared for the weather. The market is rain or shine, and since this is northern Indiana, you'll want to be ready for both. Pack all of these, just in case:

- Umbrella
- Poncho
- Sunscreen
- Sunglasses (or, you can buy some there!)
- Hat
- Cash (see above)
- Extra bags
- Cooler in your car for any cold food purchases
- Water bottle

You could also bring a wagon to make carrying your goodies easier. If you don't have one, you can rent one. Shoppers with mobility issues can rent electric scooters. Another thing to note is that, while Shipshewana Flea Market offers free admission, parking is $5, and it's cash only.

> **TLTip:** make your first stop the Information Booth near the main entrance to get a map. You can also print one from their website.

Where to Eat at Shipshewana Flea Market

Shopping builds up an appetite. Fortunately, Shipshewana Flea Market has several options. There's the Auction Restaurant, located by the entrance gate off of SR 5. Mrs. Miller may not be baking pies any more, but the dessert is still a staple. So is that Indiana favorite, the breaded pork tenderloin, and their sandwich is on the Indiana Tenderloin Lovers Trail. (The Hoosier state is *serious* about its breaded pork tenderloin.)

Within the market are several conveniently-placed food courts. These are in covered pavilions with picnic tables. There will often be live music, so you can get some entertainment with your ice cream, Port-A-Pit® Chicken Strips, and Pit-Tatoes™. There are also food trucks and several food vendors, including Ben's Pretzels, Shipshewana Sweets & Treats, and Hoosier Banquets. You can pick up some delicious Amish peanut butter at that last one. If you attend the Shipshewana Auction on Wednesday mornings, you can fill up at the Auction Barn Snack Bar.

Shipshewana Trading Place

345 S Van Buren St Shipshewana, IN 46565, 260.768.4129
shipshewanatradingplace.com

Shipshewana Miscellaneous & Antique Auction

Chaos. Barely controlled chaos. That was the first thought I had at the Shipshewana Miscellaneous & Antique Auction.

When you picture an auction, at least when I've always pictured one, it's of an orderly affair. Fast, but orderly. I haven't been to many, although I have been sold in one (for charity, of course).

Before viewing the auction at the Shipshewana Flea Market, my impression was this: People sit in their chairs and raise their paddles as the auctioneer rattles off numbers. Then the gavel bangs. "Sold!" The next item is brought to the stage and the process begins again.

The Shipshewana Auction is not like that.

It seems like chaos. Like a free-for-all. It's a bizarre bazaar. To the untrained eye, it's just a bunch of vendors hawking their wares and shouting, via amplification, over the other vendors. It's a crowded archipelago of BUY MY STUFF.

But as I learned, there is method to the madness. Lora Gates of Shipshewana Trading Place introduced me to this market, which takes place in the Antique Auction Building.

Are you curious about this auction that draws people from all over the country? Here's everything you need to know about the Shipshewana Miscellaneous and Antique Auction.

Attending the Shipshewana Auction

Rows of tables line the cavernous space. Browsers can find everything from neon signs, to children's toys, to complete sets of silver. Chinese vases. Tools. Corncob pipes. Lamps. Comic books. Rusted iron dutch ovens. A globe, and a gas can.

In the market for a slot machine from the 1940s? You might find one. Maybe an antique rocking horse would be perfect for the nursery. This would be the place to look.

Some items are obviously worth a mint. Others, like the two-foot statue of Nixon, may be considered by some to be junk, yet are destined to be someone's treasure.

Each seller, or consignor, arrives early the morning of the auction or the day before to unload and set up. Staff then photograph the items and upload the images to AuctionZip.com. Buyers can browse what's available to see if there's anything they'd be interested in before making the trip.

Consignors display their own merchandise, holding each item aloft for potential bidders as an auctioneer tries to sell it. When an item is sold, an assistant logs the information in a computer. Shipshewana Auction collects payment, and the seller receives a check for any items sold, minus commission, about an hour after their last item is auctioned off.

It sounds orderly, in the way that all auctions are a bit of a free-for-all, and it is. Now imagine this happening simultaneously with multiple sellers all over the room, and you can see why it seems like chaos.

The room is an 80-foot by 200-foot barn with concrete floors. It echoes. Add six to nine auctioneers surrounded by as many clusters of buyers shouting out bids for this huge collection of antiques, and it's a cacophony to rival a three-year-old's birthday party when the pony arrives.

You can observe, like I did, and see it's like a dance. Or you can enter the fray. A buyer number card is required. It's only $5 and expires at the end of the calendar year. Buyers have to be at least 18. The minimum opening bid is also $5, and sales tax is charged on all items.

> **TLTip:** don't even think about doing any side deals. Direct exchanges between buyers and sellers are strictly prohibited.

The Shipshewana Miscellaneous and Antique Auction takes place every Wednesday, year round, and the bell rings at 9am. In the winter, the barn is heated. In the summer, doors are opened to let fresh air flow.

All auction merchandise can be inspected prior to the auction, on Tuesdays from 7am to 5pm and Wednesdays beginning at 5:30am. However, consignors have until 7am on Wednesday to set up, so if you go Tuesday, you may not see everything. Still, you'll want to try to see as much as you can before the sound of the bell.

There are various rules for purchasing, like you have to pay that day and take your item(s) home, or you'll pay a Buyer's Premium and a storage fee. It's advised to check out their Buyer Terms before participating. Both buyers and sellers come from all over, and since items are different each week, many buyers are regulars, looking for that next great find. If you're interested in cattle, livestock auctions also take place on Wednesdays, and horse auctions are on Fridays.

Davis Mercantile

A story of community and survival

"If you want to welcome people, you give them a place to sit down."

I sat across from Alvin and Elsie Miller at Millie's Market Café on the third floor of Davis Mercantile. Across the hall, a carousel turned round and round. The smell of chocolate wafted from the candy shop next door, competing only slightly with the bacon on my turkey bacon pretzel melt.

Next to me sat Mariah Contreras, Executive Director of the

Shipshewana Retail Merchants Association, and the Millers' granddaughter.

Welcoming people is important to Alvin, Elsie, and Mariah, and not simply because it's good business. For them, it's about community.

Davis Mercantile is an anchor in downtown Shipshewana. It originally began as a hotel, built by one of the town's founders in 1891. The railroad came through in 1888, and Hezekiah Davis thought it would be a good idea to give passengers a place to stay.

He didn't live long after the Davis Hotel opened next to the tracks, but the business he established continued to welcome travelers. By the 1920s, though, the only thing remaining inside the building was a barbershop.

Over the next several decades, the Davis Hotel housed various businesses, including grain storage and a chicken hatchery. In the 1960s, the historic building's brick veneer was stripped and the frame moved up the street a couple blocks.

By the early 1980s, the building's future was uncertain. Alvin, an independent project engineer who'd previously owned a sawmill, saw Shipshewana's potential as a tourist destination.

"No one else could," he said. He'd go to nearby Middlebury, Topeka, and other towns to count cars and buggies. Which towns were busy, and when?

The Millers bought the Davis Hotel in 1982. They renovated it, returning it to its original purpose as a hotel as well as adding shops on the first floor.

One of those shops was JoJo's Pretzels. Mariah said her father named it for her mother before they were even married.

Although the railroad left in the mid-1980s, tourism grew, fueled in part by the Shipshewana Flea Market. The Millers expanded, and expanded, and expanded. Eventually, the Davis Mercantile was a mish-mash of six buildings with floors that didn't line up.

Then, in February of 2004, tragedy struck. Twice.

It was a Monday when Alvin found out he had cancer. On Saturday, Davis Mercantile burned to the ground.

There'd been a spate of unexplained fires in historic buildings in Indiana. Federal investigators arrived, including some who'd worked the Oklahoma City bombing and 9/11. While they discovered where the fire originated, they never discovered who did it.

Cancer. Fire. Someone asked Alvin how he could be so calm. "When you've got a big hole in the ground and you've got cancer, you don't want to think about cancer all the time, and you don't want to think about the hole all the time."

I can relate. I received my cancer diagnosis in August of 2020, during the height of the pandemic. My personal tragedy distracted from the global calamity, and vice versa. Instead of being overwhelming, the dual tribulations kept me from focusing on one or the other.

I have no idea why two absolutely awful things happening simultaneously, instead of one, didn't destroy my mental health and might have helped me cope, but when Alvin said that, I understood.

The Millers couldn't be on the premises for two weeks after the fire, but Alvin would still visit, walking the perimeter. A chain-link fence surrounded the hole. The devastation was nearly complete, except for the spot where Lolly's Fabrics had been. Bits of fabric laid in the ashes, somehow surviving the conflagration.

One day, Alvin came upon a woman who had her arm stretched under the fence. In her hand was a jar. He watched as she scooped up ashes and frayed, scorched cloth.

"I just wanted a little bit of Lolly's," she said.

The Millers may have had an inkling about the impact Davis Mercantile had on the community, but that woman's desire to preserve a piece of it was tangible evidence.

"To build something like that is really special," Alvin said. "Can we duplicate what was here?"

"Little did we know what help we'd get," Elsie said.

Throughout all this, Alvin was dealing with his cancer. It was a cancer that would require surgery, which meant travel to Ohio to get the proper care. How could he rebuild while trying to fight the disease?

With community. By September of that year, not only had Alvin recovered from surgery and beat cancer, but they also had an old-fashioned barn-raising. So many people showed up to help, they had trouble finding them all work.

This type of community support is the norm in Shipshewana and LaGrange County, which has the third largest Amish population in the country. Still, even though it might have been expected, it wasn't taken for granted.

The Millers wanted to create a place where people could feel welcome. Yes, they said, they wanted visitors to buy something eventually, but that wasn't the first thing they thought of.

That year, the Millers had lots of family meetings. One big question was how to make it more kid-friendly, and how to bring people to the third floor. One of Mariah's cousins suggested a slide, but as Elsie said, that would separate children from their parents.

They settled on a carousel, finding antique frameworks abandoned in a barn. "They were bedded down just like you'd bed down cattle," Elsie said.

One family member suggested a candy store. The youngest thought a toy store would be a good idea. Elsie figured they'd need a place to eat.

The carousel is now one of the top attractions in Shipshewana. Its gears and inner workings are open. It's in keeping with the community itself, illustrating workmanship and the simple beauty of engineering without ornamentation. The animals, carved by an Amish man, are horses and farm animals. The benches are buggy seats.

The entire Davis Mercantile building is accessible, including the carousel. And true to Alvin's belief in welcoming people, there are places to sit down nearly everywhere you look.

Besides the carousel, the most interesting feature of Davis Mercantile is its staircase. Made of tulip poplar, cherry, beech, and maple, all native hardwoods, it's a work of art. Alvin, the former engineer and sawmill owner, designed it.

At each landing are pieces of the Millers' and Shipshewana's history. This staircase isn't just about getting from one floor to another. It's a living gallery, and its centerpiece is a gigantic tree.

This "One Large Log," as it was described on the packing list, is a Douglas Fir from British Columbia. It's over 370 years old, is 56-feet tall. and more than 44-inches in diameter.

It's impressive.

Why did Alvin want to put a giant tree in the middle of the building? Basically, because he knew it would draw attention, and it has. There are two elevators, one on either side of the building. Before the fire, about 80% of visitors used the elevators. After the fire, with the new arboreal centerpiece, that number dropped to 25%.

This change makes visiting Davis Mercantile a more intentional experience. Shoppers take their time and browse the four floors filled with 21 shops and eateries, including JoJo's Pretzels and Lolly's Fabrics.

> **TLTip:** Sarah Davis, a women's apparel shop, is named for Hezekiah Davis's wife.

A December 2004 article in the South Bend Tribune reported on the fire and the building-raising frolic. It began with this:

> "Alvin and Elsie Miller have a lot of friends."

Yes, they do. They've got a whole community.

Davis Mercantile

225 N Harrison St Shipshewana, IN 46565, 260.768.7300
davismercantile.com

The Art of Quilting

In a community whose main tenets include humility, it's fitting that its art is functional. The Amish are known for their well-crafted furniture, and they're also known for their quilts.

Although quilting is an ancient practice, the Amish didn't adopt it until the 1870s. But when they adopt something, they go all-in. At the time, quilting was fairly modern, and since the Amish eschew modern life, the decision to allow this form of expression only happened after discussion. Considerations on the overall quality of life and how a new–to them–practice would impact their community were hashed out, and it was decided that quilts were acceptable.

Creating a quilt is an intentional act, especially when intricate designs are used. It's more than just sewing some material together. There's backing, and batting, and the design itself. The finished product is beautiful, with a story woven into its threads.

Quilts are functional because they're incredibly warm, their multiple layers serving to trap body heat. I learned this after we received a quilt as a gift while visiting my in-laws in California. On our drive back to Illinois, we camped in southern Utah. It was March, and it was cold. Below-freezing cold, and we were in a tent. Yet we stayed warm because we had that quilt. I've been a fan ever since.

For the Amish, quilting is an integral part of their socialization. Quilting bees invite the women and girls to gather around, working on a project together. The skill is learned from an early age.

And it is a skill. It is an art.

Up until the early 1970s, to the general public, quilts were just quilts. You put them on beds. But then the Whitney Museum in New York City had an exhibit displaying quilts on walls. *Abstract Design in American Quilts* was a huge success and it transformed the way people saw quilts.

This began to draw attention to the handiwork, the craft, and the art of Amish quilts. Rebecca Haarer, who grew up in Shipshewana and received a BA in Art Education from nearby Goshen College, became fascinated by this art form. Descended from both Mennonite and Amish, she took a break from teaching in the late 1970s to study the latter. At the time, Shipshewana was not a tourist destination. There were no gift shops, nothing to attract visitors. During this break, Rebecca would travel to farm auctions with her father, an antique dealer and owner of Haarer's Quaint Shop. She moved into an Amish "grandmother house," as she called it. Also known as a Dawdi Haus, it's a separate house built on a farm to keep the family together. It works great as the younger generation has kids; the grandparents are right there to help out.

Rebecca's move to one of these homes inspired passion, and she "unintentionally became a collector of Amish and Mennonite" quilts. When you visit Shipshewana, you can see many of these historic works of art at Rebecca Haarer Arts and Antiques, her father's former shop. Rebecca also presents these quilts at what she calls Trunk Shows. Check her Facebook page to find upcoming events. She can also arrange a combined lecture and dinner at an Amish farm.

Rebecca Haarer Arts and Antiques

65 Morton St Shipshewana, IN 46565, 260.768.4787

A GALLERY OF
AMISH QUILTS
Design Diversity from a Plain People
ROBERT BISHOP and ELIZABETH SAFANDA

Please, let us help
with those old
textiles.

Downtown Shipshewana

Shipshewana's tiny. Not just its population, but also its size. According to the 2010 census, the entire town is only 1.18 square miles. Some sources claim it's even smaller. Which, if you're in the mood for shopping, is great news.

As you stroll around downtown (which, in a town that size, is basically *the* town), the sheer number of shops is mind-boggling. There's the Davis Mercantile, with its four stories of retailers, and there are also several boutiques lining the streets. Considering the Shipshewana Flea Market is the town's claim to fame (besides its Amish residents), it makes sense that shopping is one of its biggest attractions.

The main shopping drags are Harrison Street and Morton Street. There are antique, clothing, home goods, and quilting shops, and furniture stores.

There are also bakeries, including the Blue Gate Bakery, located inside Blue Gate Restaurant and Theater. South of downtown, a whopping one-tenth of a mile, is Yoder's Shopping Center. You'll see the Yoder name on several businesses, including Yoder Popcorn, Yoder's Meat & Cheese, and Yoder's Red Barn Shoppes. Those last two are just south of the flea market on Van Buren Street (SR 5).

There's also Next Door Shops, which is where you'll find the La-Grange County Visitor's Center. Before you start strolling, stop by and pick up a walking map of downtown. Not only will it help you figure out where to go, you might find a coupon.

More Shopping

While Shipshewana's a hive of shopping activity, you can get your retail therapy all over the county. Whether you're drawn to the charm of Amish cottage industry shops, the bustling atmosphere of a wholesale food market, or the unique finds sprinkled throughout the county, you'll discover it all here.

Make sure you bring cash or your checkbook. Many Amish-owned businesses do not accept credit cards. Also remember that these businesses will be closed on Sundays.

This is a very abbreviated selection of shops, and is more to give you an idea of the types of retail options you'll have. For more thorough information, request a visitor's guide from LaGrange County Visitor's Bureau and visit their website at visitshipshewana.org.

Amish Cottage Industry Shops

As you're driving the back roads of LaGrange County, keep your eyes peeled for signs advertising goods. These are known as "shingle shops," so named because they hang a shingle on the side of the road. You can find a whole variety of products, including baked goods and quilts. And, as Rebecca Haarer said, "if you see a sign that says 'eggs for sale,' go buy some."

Quilt and Fabric Shops

If you're a quilter, or interested in learning, you've hit the jackpot. Quilting shops can be found all over the county, but primarily in Shipshewana. Downtown you'll find Lolly's Fabrics inside Davis Mercantile and Rebecca Haarer Arts and Antiques on Morton Street. You can pick up a brochure listing area shops at the visitor's center.

Silver Star Leather

For all things leather, visit this shop north of Shipshewana. They carry everything from belts to leather-bound journals. In addition to standard hides, they also have exotic leathers, including alligator and ostrich. You can buy pre-made products, made by hand by Amish crafters, or you can custom order. They'll even size a computer bag to fit your laptop, or make your handmade leather purse. Curious about how these are made? Take a tour of their solar-powered workshop.
6875 N 800 W Shipshewana, IN 46565, 260.768.7958
silverstarleather.com

"B" Honey

Operating since 1986, "B" Honey in Shipshewana offers more than just honey. Most products are crafted on-site, including regular and flavored honey, pure beeswax candles, and skincare items. They also stock hand-sewn décor and an array of jams and jellies.
2260 N 1000 W Shipshewana, IN 46565, 574.642.1145

Lehman's Variety Store

Lehman's Variety Store is aptly named; it's got a huge variety of goods on its shelves. Catering to the Amish, there are hats, kapps (women's bonnets), pants, jackets, and vests. While the pants and jackets are black, the shirts and dresses come in a variety of colors. There are shoes, and the community favors Skechers and Crocs (or shoes similar to Crocs).

The store carries more than clothing, however. You'll find battery-operated kitchen appliances, battery-operated fans, toys, books, canning supplies, linens—pretty much everything you'd need to supply a house in the country. Lehman's is on a dirt road behind a farmhouse. There's a sign, but it's easy to miss.
2795 W 350 S LaGrange, IN 46761, 260.463.7469

E & S Sales

Just south of the Shipshewana Flea Market, E & S Sales is easy to find. The store offers an expansive range of bulk foods—from cold cut meats and an array of cheeses to home-style noodles made on-site. Shoppers can also find a comprehensive selection of baking essentials such as spices, nuts, and flours, along with a variety of jams, jellies, and snacks. Fresh produce and freshly baked items round out the offerings, making it a one-stop shop.
1265 N SR 5 Shipshewana, IN 46565, 260.768.4736

EASH Sales

Next door to E & S Sales is EASH Sales, open since 1975. This is the place to go if you're looking for gazebos, storage sheds, porch swings, and appliances. You can even buy non-electric kitchen tools, off-grid lighting, hammocks, and log cabins.
1205 N SR 5 Shipshewana, IN 46565, 260.768.7511
eashsalespolyoutdoorfurniture.com

Yoder Department Store

Yoder Department Store began in 1945 when Ora and Grace Yoder bought a dry goods store in Topeka. Originally focused on products for the farming community, they grew quickly, opening a Shipshewana location in 1952. After consolidating, Ora decided to move the store "out of town," or just south of downtown.

Today, that store is the focal point of Yoder Shopping Center, which also includes Yoder's Hardware and The Cotton Corner. They specialize in fabric, shoes, and clothing, and their employees are trained to help you coordinate materials for your quilting projects and to fit shoes properly.

300 S Van Buren St Shipshewana, IN 46565, 260.768.4887
yoderdepartmentstore.com

BILL McCONNEL
REYNOLDS ILL.
HAMILTON
GREYHOUND
ball bearing

Arts & Entertainment

Overview

Shipshewana's entertainment scene is vibrant and a perfect encapsulation of this complex area. There are live performances at the intimate Blue Gate Music Hall, including Amish-themed musicals. Big names take the stage at the Blue Gate Performing Arts Center, and the Michiana Event Center is a hub for auctions, equine events, rodeos, and more.

Art is on public display with several murals in LaGrange County's communities, especially the series painted by the Walldogs. There are also many barn quilts, which you can discover while taking one of the driving tours.

Pictured: Carpenters Once More at Blue Gate Music Hall

Blue Gate Music Hall and Blue Gate Performing Arts Center

When you're in Shipshewana, don't limit your visit to just the auction, flea market, and food. Make sure you set aside time for live entertainment at the Blue Gate Music Hall and the Blue Gate Performing Arts Center.

Located conveniently above the Blue Gate Restaurant, the Blue Gate Music Hall seats 325 and specializes in Broadway-style musicals that pay tribute to the rich culture of Amish Country. It's a unique blend, this marriage of urban art form and rural storytelling. Imagine hearing an Amish love tale set to a Broadway score. Sounds curious, doesn't it? But that's the charm. There are also concerts, and in this intimate space, there isn't a bad spot in the house.

Down the road next to Blue Gate Garden Inn, the Blue Gate Performing Arts Center (PAC) is where the big artists come to play. Formerly the Shipshewana Event Center, the Riegseckers, who own Blue Gate Hospitality Group, rebuilt the space and it's now a 1500-seat venue. It attracts nationally touring artists like Marina McBride, Marie Osmond, and STYX.

Designed to look like a barn from the outside, on the inside, the entrance to the PAC is lined with a hodge-podge of memorabilia. There's barely any open space on the walls with all the guitars and concert posters. There are old gas pumps and antique vehicles, a leftover from the space's days as the Hudson Auto Museum. There's also a mural painted by the Walldogs, the traveling artists that created several murals in downtown Shipshewana.

Part of the conversion to the PAC was including a convention center which can host up to 1200 people. And because it's Blue Gate, you know the catering will be good.

Event schedule and tickets for both venues are at thebluegate.com.

Blue Gate Music Hall

175 N Van Buren St Shipshewana, IN 46565, 260.768.4725

Blue Gate Performing Arts Center

760 S Van Buren St Shipshewana, IN 46565, 260.768.4725

Michiana Event Center

The Michiana Event Center, commonly known as the MEC, is a key entertainment venue in LaGrange County. The center's coliseum can seat up to 6,000 people, accommodating a diverse line-up of events, and they've got a 100,000 square foot trade show area.

With those spaces, the MEC hosts a broad range of events and expos. They host several equine events, like the North American Clydesdale/Shire Fall Classic, The Equine Expo, and rodeos. There are also auctions of all types, including crafts, horses, and RVs.

Check their calendar for all upcoming events.

Michiana Event Center

455 E Farver St Shipshewana, IN 46565, 260.768.3300
michianaevents.com

MURALS OF LAGRANGE COUNTY

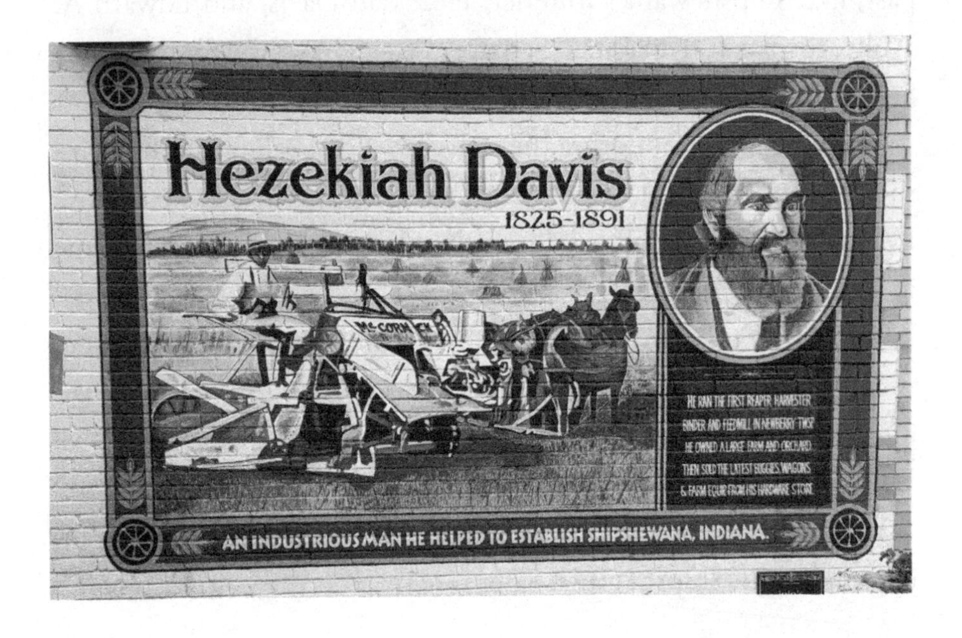

If you're from the Midwest, or have driven through a few small towns, you might have noticed that murals have become increasingly popular. Towns like Dubuque, Iowa; Plymouth, Wisconsin; and Pontiac, Illinois are a miniscule sampling of communities who have turned bland buildings into works of art.

So has Shipshewana.

Many of these murals are painted by a group called Walldogs, a collection of talented muralists who travel the country to make it more beautiful. Not only are these murals attractive, they also tell the stories of the communities.

Walldogs came to Shipshewana in 2014. The collection of sixteen murals they created introduce you to important figures in the area's past, like Shipshewana's founder, Hezekiah Davis, and Edward A. Wolfe, former Indiana State Senator, President of the Shipshewana State Bank, and businessman.

There's a mural honoring the short-lived baseball team, the Shipshewana Indians, and another one featuring Pletchers Pacing Acres. Lester Pletcher was inducted into the Harness Horse Hall of Fame in Indiana and Illinois.

These aren't the only murals in town. Stroll through the Shipshewana Flea Market and you'll see a few that were added in 2023. Over in the county seat of LaGrange are even more, as well as in Howe. Each one helps to bring the past to life.

You can take a self-guided walking tour to view most of the Walldogs murals in Shipshewana. There are maps at the visitor's center.

Dining in LaGrange County

Overview

You won't go hungry in Amish Country

Pack your stretchy pants for your visit to Shipshewana, because when you eat in Amish Country, you won't go hungry. The area's known for hearty cuisine and generous portions. The rich flavors reflect a culture that values simplicity, family, and tradition. Prepared from whole ingredients, the food is a testament to a way of life that emphasizes quality and connection to the land. From homemade breads and jams to robust stews and pies, each dish is an invitation to savor not just a meal, but a piece of heritage.

One of the best ways to experience this is by dining in an Amish home, and I had the pleasure of doing so. There are also plenty of choices when you want to explore other culinary options, and this chapter will help you find them.

Blue Gate Restaurant and Bakery

If you've heard of Shipshewana, you've probably heard of Blue Gate Restaurant and Bakery. The dining room can seat almost as many people as the town has residents, and the bakery has more varieties of pie and baked goods than you could finish in a month.

And it all began with a miniature wagon drawn by miniature horses.

Mel Riegsecker started carving as a hobby while working in the RV industry. His father, an Amish man who made and repaired harnesses for their neighbors, displayed Mel's tiny wagon and six intricately detailed horses in his shop. It didn't take long before someone bought it. Mel kept carving, and then a buyer from a large department store in Chicago found his work. Demand exploded, and people wanted to see the artisan who crafted these sculptures.

At first, visitors would watch Mel carve in the workshop next to his home. That got to be so popular that he and his wife, June, decided to expand. They bought an old factory building and renamed it the Shipshewana Craft Barn.

Out of that modest beginning, the Blue Gate Hospitality Company was born. Today's company covers nearly every aspect of a visit to Shipshewana. There's Blue Gate Garden Inn if you're looking for a place to sleep; Blue Gate Theater and Performing Arts Center for entertainment; several stores, including the Shipshewana Craft Barn; and Blue Gate Restaurant and Bakery.

The restaurant began in the mid-1980s as Der Strudel Haus and only sat 50 people. They kept expanding, but so did the demand. After twenty years, Mel and June tore down the old spot and built a place that could seat 750 people, with six dining rooms, a bakery, and upstairs, a theater.

The Blue Gate Restaurant specializes in home-style Amish cuisine. You can order off the menu or go all-in with one of their buffets. Signature items include Blue Gate Fried Chicken (highly, highly recommend), roast beef, mashed potatoes, noodles, beans, corn, and other hearty options. It's basically an all-you-can-eat homage to comfort food, Midwest-style.

If you're going for something lighter, they've got entrée salads. On the menu, one of the "Lighter Options" is the Mennonite Delight:

chicken salad, fruit, cottage cheese, potato salad, and a garden salad.

Dessert, of course, is pie. While the cherry pie is great, my personal favorite is the red raspberry cream pie. That's a smile on a plate.

No matter what you order, you're in for an experience that goes beyond just a meal, especially if you've booked tickets for a show at the upstairs theater.

There's a reason Blue Gate is a cornerstone of Shipshewana hospitality. Reservations are recommended, especially if you're visiting during flea market days.

Blue Gate Restaurant and Bakery

195 N Van Buren St Shipshewana, IN 46565, 260.768.4725
thebluegate.com

DINNER IN AN AMISH HOME

We were almost late.

Karleen, from Visit Shipshewana, picked me up at the Blue Gate Garden Inn for dinner with the Amish. She'd arrived right on time, but our drive to The Carriage House in Topeka was filled with distractions and we drove slowly, a necessity in Amish country, and pulled over frequently.

It had been a hot, humid day, and in the early evening, haze and clouds blurred the sun and gave tree-lined lanes a sense of mystery. We drove past a school with an old-fashioned merry-go-round, the kind I spent countless hours spinning in the '70s. We stopped to take photos. A little further down the road, a farmer tilled his field with a horse-drawn plow. We pulled over to watch him work. Two carriages clip-clopped past. I took video, careful not to point my lens inside the carriages so I wouldn't capture the people inside.

> **TLTip:** Amish people do not want their photographs taken. If you do want to take photos of them, make sure no faces are included in the image. And always ask.

We resumed our journey, and I noticed well-kept sheds with RV doors on the side of the road. Amish phone booths, Karleen explained. We passed one as we turned into a driveway. A Clydesdale munched on grass and I jumped out to say hello before we drove past a two-story farmhouse and a row of evergreens towards the parking lot. A tour bus took up most of the space in the gravel lot. Although dinner was about to start, there were horses, and I can never *not* stop to say hi to horses.

Across from the house sat a rectangular one-story building. We finally entered, and it was packed; every seat but two was filled and we took our places. I wasn't sure what to expect. This was to be my first Amish wedding feast. I knew there would be an inordinate amount of food because I'd checked the menu for The Carriage House ahead of time. What they feed one person is enough to feed a family of four.

Quilts lined the walls of the expansive space. There had to have been a hundred people there, seated in folding chairs at long rows of white-clothed tables. I later learned they were from Michigan's Upper Peninsula. We were all there to learn more about a way of life that's entirely different from anything any of us experience.

And to eat a *lot* of food.

The Carriage House is run by a mother and son team. Elaine and Seth serve authentic Amish dinners in their former carriage house. The farmhouse we passed was Elaine's. The Clydesdale was Seth's. We were in their home.

The evening began with a crash course on Amish weddings. Seth asked how many people we thought attended these affairs. People guessed. 400? 500?

Not even close.

1,000 to 1,200 people attend a typical–*typical*–Amish wedding. One of the young ladies who served us said she was attending thirteen this year. Amish weddings are well-oiled machines, which should come as no surprise to anyone who knows the work ethic of their culture. Everyone doesn't attend at once, however. They appear in waves. About 500 or so attend the wedding ceremony, which begins at 9am with the wedding happening at 11:30am.

Seth, a thin man wearing standard Amish attire, explained how dozens of cooks would prepare the meals. Cooking at a wedding is done by women and it's considered an honor. Their husbands will often help, willingly, because of the promise of extra mashed potatoes.

If you haven't had Amish mashed potatoes, stop whatever you're doing and get some. Find a recipe. Go to Shipshewana. You'll thank me, I promise.

Seth, who married in 2014 ("still a newlywed"), displayed his wife's wedding dress. Like the rest of her clothing, a bride's wedding dress is simple, and she'll make it herself. He told us bout how Amish see marriage. "Marriage is a triangle: God, Bride, Groom." There are no notes during the sermon, which is in German or Pennsylvania Dutch. "God leads what his people need," Seth explained.

Their faith is what drives them, but later I overheard him say that being "Amish is not a religion. It's a way of life."

Before the young ladies served dinner, Seth treated us to a small portion of the German Wedding song. The full version takes twenty minutes and is sung at every Amish wedding.

Dinner–oh, that dinner. Course after course of hearty, wholesome food. Baskets of soft wheat bread sat every few feet, alternating with pitchers of ice water and coffee and crocks of Amish peanut butter, a distinctively sweet spread enhanced with marshmallow cream, corn syrup, and butter.

A trio of young women served us family-style. First the salad, with Elaine's signature dressing made with Miracle Whip–it must be Miracle Whip–and her special champagne vinegar. The Amish don't consume alcohol; this vinegar is made with champagne grapes.

Meatloaf, roasted pork with barbecue sauce, green beans, noodles, stuffing, and mashed potatoes made the rounds. It was like Thanksgiving dinner without the turkey. Every bite was delicious, especially those creamy, rich mashed potatoes. And then there was cake and two kinds of pie: banana cream and my husband's favorite, cherry. I brought him back a piece. Mistake, because now I really need to up my pie game.

Now, imagine serving all of that to a thousand people. The sheer quantity of ingredients is mind-boggling. Seth said they've got a wedding cookbook. Those mashed potatoes? That recipe calls for

400 pounds of spuds and 20 bars of cream cheese.

Cooking all that food requires two head cooks, who are essentially project managers. The wedding cake is decorated with flowers, and there are bowls of cookies, which are shared with guests who help the new couple move.

And what about clean-up? Well, they swear by the three Ps: paper, plastic, pitch.

Weddings usually take place on Thursdays. Clean up is Friday, and the couple moves on Saturday.

The Carriage House has expanded over the years. Seth used to have to escort diners to the main house if they needed to use the facilities. Now, there are men's and women's bathrooms. The kitchen is commercial grade. In fact, they're one of the few licensed Amish kitchens in the area.

Those quilts that line the walls? Elaine made them. All of them. "This is how I relax," she said. She loves the feel of cotton. The designs range from historic patterns to modern. They're all different sizes, including pot holders.

All of them are for sale. They also sell that champagne vinegar that makes her salad dressing so good, as well as apple butter, peanut butter, baskets, horseshoes, and birdhouses roofed with buggy license plates.

After dinner, Karleen and I visited the horses again before sitting down with Elaine. She explained how she and her son made a good combination. At the end of the day, "He goes home to his wife. I go home to my husband."

There aren't a lot of things I say are "must-dos," because I believe everyone defines their *musts* differently. However, if you're visiting Shipshewana and LaGrange County, you're most likely there because of the intrigue and allure of the Amish community.

Dinner with the Amish, especially at The Carriage House, is an experience you won't want to miss.

And when you go, say hi to the horsies and save some of those mashed potatoes for me.

The Carriage House

5280 S 500 W Topeka, IN 46571, 260.768.8199

Shipshewana Auction Restaurant

If you're in Shipshewana for the auction and flea market, do yourself a favor and stop at the Shipshewana Auction Restaurant. It's right next to the action, making it an easy stop between rounds of bargaining.

The menu is a mix of Amish favorites and classic American comfort food. Think fried chicken that's crispy and juicy. And don't even get me started on the pies—apple and rhubarb are the stars here. Best part? Most of the ingredients come from local farms, so you're getting a real taste of the area.

The restaurant is more than just a spot to refuel. On auction days, it's like the town square, buzzing with energy. People come to chat about the deals they scored or the rare finds they spotted. It's part of the whole Shipshewana experience, blending food, community, and a touch of nostalgia.

You don't have to shop at the Shipshewana Flea Market or the auction to dine at their on-site restaurant. However, this popular spot is only open on Tuesdays, Wednesdays, and Fridays during Flea Market & Auction hours and special events. If you do go, try the pork tenderloin sandwich; it's on the Indiana Foodways Alliance's Tenderloin Lover's Trail for a reason.

Shipshewana Auction Restaurant

345 S Van Buren St Shipshewana, IN 46565, 260.336.8362
shipshewanatradingplace.com/restaurant

More Dining

There's more than mashed potatoes in LaGrange County. Expect lots of spots for burgers, pizza, and of course, pie.

Once you get outside of Shipshewana, you'll find more restaurants open on Sundays. If you're making a weekend trip of it, be sure to confirm their hours before heading out to eat.

I've listed a few spots, but there are plenty more places to eat in LaGrange County. For several dining options, request a visitor's guide from LaGrange County Visitor's Bureau and visit their website at visitshipshewana.org.

Howe

Howe Restaurant

Howe Family Restaurant is known for its warm hospitality and tasty meals. Enjoy breakfast any time of day, take advantage of daily specials, or indulge in a slice of homemade pie. Offers a variety of burgers, sandwiches, and pizza.

SR 9 & SR 120, Howe, IN 46746, 260.562.3132

LaGrange

Destination 814

This restaurant's industrial feel is just right for their scratch kitchen and extensive bourbon selection. Destination 814 is known for burgers and sandwiches, but don't miss the pork-n-pickles.
814 S Detroit St LaGrange, IN 46761, 260.214.5612
destination814bar.com

Fireside Craft Burgers & Brews

Across the street from the historic LaGrange County Courthouse, Fireside Craft Burgers & Brews is exactly what it sounds like. Expect Angus burgers with toppings like garlic aioli and smoked mushrooms. In addition to craft beers, they've also got specialty cocktails.
101 S Detroit St LaGrange, IN 46761, 260.768.3473
firesideindiana.com

Mongo

Mongo General Store

Before hunting, fishing, or kayaking, fill up at Mongo General Store. This one-pump gas station, which is also the village post office, is known for its pork burger.

3000 N SR 3 Mongo, IN 46771, 260.367.2442

Shipshewana

East of Chicago Pizza

If you're hankering for pizza, there's a spot right on Shipshewana's main drag. East of Chicago Pizza has several types of crust, including, of course, Chicago-style. They've also got salads, oven baked subs, and wings, plus a slew of appetizers.
350 S Van Buren St Shipshewana, IN 46565, 260.768.7272
eastofchicago.com

Topeka

Tiffany's Restaurant

Located in the heart of Amish country, Tiffany's Restaurant serves comfort food: hearty breakfasts, quick lunches, and mouthwatering dinners. You'll be welcomed by a friendly staff and tempted by an array of pies and desserts.
414 E Lake St Topeka, IN 46571, 260.593.2988
tiffanystopeka.com

Wolcottville

Coody Brown's Lakeside Grill

Pescetarians will love Coody Brown's. Located between Westler and Witmer Lakes, with docks as well as a parking lot, their menu highlights plenty of seafood. They're also known for their wings. If the weather's nice, snag a seat on their waterside deck.
1510 E 700 S Wolcottville, IN 46795, 260.854.2425

Southfork

EXTEND YOUR TRIP

THINGS TO DO IN THE SURROUNDING AREAS

After soaking in LaGrange County, why not see what else is nearby? The region is filled with outdoor adventures, historical landmarks, and unique shopping experiences.

Das Dutchman Essenhaus

Classic Amish cooking and a nostalgic setting with a weekly seasonal classic car show.
240 US-20, Middlebury, IN 46540, (800) 455-9471
essenhaus.com

Gene Stratton-Porter State Historic Site

Honor the life and works of this iconic naturalist and Indiana's most widely-read female author.
1205 Pleasant Point, Rome City, IN 46784, 260.854.3790
indianamuseum.org

Midwest Museum of American Art

Hosting a comprehensive collection of 19th – 21st-century American art.
429 S Main St, Elkhart, IN 46516, 574.293.6660
midwestmuseum.org

Heritage Trail

An audio driving tour showcasing the Amish and Mennonite lifestyles.
800.262.8161 visitelkhartcounty.com/things-to-do/heritage-trail

Quilt Gardens Trail

Garden spots in Elkhart County display quilt patterns in flower arrangements.
800.262.8161 quiltgardens.com

Where to Stay

LaGrange County may not be swimming in hotels, but it does have a variety of places to stay. There are locally owned inns, bed and breakfasts, and campgrounds and cabins, as well as a few chain hotels. Below is a variety of recommended accommodations. For more options, check out visitshipshewana.org.

Blue Gate Garden Inn

One of the most popular hotels is the comfortable Blue Gate Garden Inn. It's part of the Blue Gate Hospitality Group, which you've already met through their restaurant, bakery, and performance spaces.

Shipshewana is a family-friendly destination, and nowhere is that more evident than at Blue Gate. This resort-like hotel is designed to be more than just a place to sleep. It's a place to gather. There are seating areas sprinkled throughout the hotel. Turn a corner and there's another cluster of couches. There's also a large indoor swimming pool with a hot tub, an arcade, and a spacious outdoor patio with a fire pit. To enjoy the latter, claim a seat early, if you can. During my stay, the fire pit was decidedly popular.

Fitness buffs will love the basketball and tetherball courts, as well as the fitness center. After you've burned the calories, get a well-deserved treat at The Ice Creamery (which also serves pizza). The décor is old-fashioned, and there's even a buggy outfitted for dining.

Your stay comes with a complimentary breakfast buffet, and this is where being under the Blue Gate umbrella shines: the morning pastries are from the Blue Gate Bakery. You can also get custom-ordered omelets. If you're there on a day when biscuits and gravy is an option, get it. This former (once and always) Hoosier can verify that it's some of the best sausage gravy around. I didn't even need to add any pepper.

The rooms are large and there are several configurations that will accommodate groups from three to eight. All rooms come with a microwave and a refrigerator, which come in handy when you have leftovers from that big Amish dinner and bought some pie to take home.

The Blue Gate Garden Inn is located next to the Performing Arts Center, making it super convenient if you plan to see a show. It's a five-minute drive to downtown Shipshewana, unless you get behind a buggy, which will happen. If so, take your time. It's all part of the Shipshewana experience.

800 S Van Buren St, Shipshewana, IN 46565, 888.447.4725
bluegategardeninn.com

Additional places to stay:

Essenhouse Inn & Conference Center

Located in neighboring Elkhart County, this complex includes the popular Das Dutchman Essenhaus restaurant as well as boutiques in what were once homestead buildings. This is an alcohol-free campus, including BYO.
240 US Hwy 20 Middlebury, IN 46540, 574.825.9471
essenhaus.com

The Farmstead Inn & Conference Center

Inspired by a traditional Amish farmstead, this spot provides unique touches like a ping-pong room and an indoor 1/4 basketball court.
370 S Van Buren St Shipshewana, IN 46565, 260.768.4595
farmsteadinn.com

The Morton House

Feel like you've come home after a long day at this 19th-century inn. Your stay will be "un-hosted," meaning you'll check in and out on your own.
100 N Morton St Shipshewana, IN 46565, 574.238.5559
shipshewanalodging.com

Shipshewana Trading Place RV Park & Service Center

If you're an RVer planning on going to the flea market, you can't get any closer than this on-site spot.
510 E Farver St Shipshewana, IN 46565, 260.768.7627
shipshewanatradingplace.com/rv

Trading Post Outfitters

With riverside spots for both tents and RVs, this is a great place to camp if you plan to have some outdoor adventures.
7525 E 300 N Mongo, IN 46771, 260.367.2493
tradingpostcanoe.com/camping

Van Buren Hotel at Shipshewana

Located north of downtown Shipshewana, this comfortable hotel has a fireplace in the lobby, an indoor pool, and breakfast is included.
1175 N Van Buren St Shipshewana, IN 46565, 855.768.7780
vanburenhotel.com

Plan your Adventure

Plan Your Adventure

Ready to plan your trip to Indiana Amish Country? These planning pages will help you stay organized and keep all your information in one place. There are also journal pages at the back so you can record your memories.

To print these and find even more planning pages, including daily schedule and daily budget, visit *thelocaltourist.com/shipshe-planning*

Included:

- Pre-Trip Checklist
- Accommodations Research Worksheet
- Attractions Research Worksheet
- Restaurants Research Worksheet
- Itinerary
- Attractions
- Restaurants
- Budget

PRE-TRIP CHECKLIST

- ⬡ Book accommodations
- ⬡ Book attractions
- ⬡ Make restaurant reservations
- ⬡ Let someone know about trip: ____________________
- ⬡ Arrange plant care: ____________________
- ⬡ Arrange pet care: ____________________
- ⬡ Share itinerary with: ____________________
- ⬡ Share location with : ____________________
- ⬡ Print itinerary & confirmation numbers
- ⬡ Put lights on a timer
- ⬡ Program thermostat
- ⬡ Put mail and paper on hold
- ⬡ Clean out refrigerator/freezer
- ⬡ Put small item on cup of ice
- ⬡ Create ice block(s) for cooler
- ⬡ Take out trash
- ⬡ Lock windows and doors
- ⬡ Unplug small appliances
- ⬡ Get vehicle inspected
- ⬡ Download music, etc.
- ⬡ Download apps
- ⬡ Set up auto-backup for phone
- ⬡ Check for tolls
- ⬡ Map route
- ⬡ Paper maps

NOTES

ACCOMMODATIONS RESEARCH

Write down your potential accommodations and list their estimated costs, pros, and cons.

Accommodations	$$	Pros	Cons

ATTRACTIONS RESEARCH

Write down potential attractions, activities, museums, etc. and list their estimated costs, pros, and cons.

Attractions	$$	Pros	Cons

RESTAURANTS RESEARCH

Write down potential restaurants and dining options and list their estimated costs, pros, and cons.

Restaurants	$$	Pros	Cons

BUDGET

Trip Budget: ____________ Total Spent: ____________

Transportation	Budget	Actual	+/-
Gas			
Vehicle - rental or maintenance			
Tolls			
Misc			
TOTAL			

Accommodations	Budget	Actual	+/-
TOTAL			

Meals & Activities	Budget	Actual	+/-
Food & Drink			
Activities & Attractions			
Souvenirs			
Misc			
TOTAL			

Pre-trip Expenses	Budget	Actual	+/-
TOTAL			

Notes

ITINERARY

From: ______________________ To: ______________________

Accommodations

Name ______________________ Phone ______________

Address ______________________________________

Website ______________________ Confirmation ____________

Day ____________ Date ____________

Day ____________ Date ____________

Day ____________ Date ____________

Day ____________ Date ____________

ITINERARY

Day ________________ Date ________________

Day ________________ Date ________________

Day ________________ Date ________________

Day ________________ Date ________________

Day ________________ Date ________________

Day ________________ Date ________________

ATTRACTIONS

Name ______ Phone ______ Date ______

Address ______ Hours ______

Website ______ Tickets ______

Notes

Name ______ Phone ______ Date ______

Address ______ Hours ______

Website ______ Tickets ______

Notes

Name ______ Phone ______ Date ______

Address ______ Hours ______

Website ______ Tickets ______

Notes

Name ______ Phone ______ Date ______

Address ______ Hours ______

Website ______ Tickets ______

Notes

RESTAURANTS

Name ______________________ Phone ______________ Date ____________

Address ______________________________ Reservation ____________

Website ___________________________

Notes

Name ______________________ Phone ______________ Date ____________

Address ______________________________ Reservation ____________

Website ___________________________

Notes

Name ______________________ Phone ______________ Date ____________

Address ______________________________ Reservation ____________

Website ___________________________

Notes

Name ______________________ Phone ______________ Date ____________

Address ______________________________ Reservation ____________

Website ___________________________

Notes